Lifelines 34

Darwin
An illustrated life of Charles Darwin
1809-1882
F. D. Fletcher

Shire Publications Ltd

Contents

ACKNOWLEDGEMENTS

Illustrations are acknowledged as follows: British Museum, page 39; Radio Times Hulton Picture Library, pages 7, 23, 31; Royal College of Surgeons of England, Medical Illustration Unit, pages 4 (top and bottom), 8, 11, 27, 29, 40, 42; Thames & Hudson, pages 35, 43. The illustrations on pages 15, 19 (top and bottom), 21 (top and bottom) are from the 'Narrative of the Surveying Voyages of His Majesty's Ships Adventure and Beagle between the Years 1826 and 1836'. The maps on pages 12-13 and 16 are by R. G. Holmes. The cover shows a map of the Galapagos Islands. The publishers acknowledge with gratitude the assistance of Mr P. Titheridge, Custodian, the Darwin Memorial, The Royal College of Surgeons of England.

Printed in Great Britain by C. I. Thomas & Sons (Haverfordwest) Ltd, Press Buildings, Merlins Bridge, Haverfordwest.

(Facing page) Charles Darwin in old age.

(Above) The Mount, Shrewsbury, home of Dr Robert Darwin and birthplace of his son Charles.

(Right) Dr Robert Darwin, Charles's father, was determined that his son should follow him in the medical profession.

Early life and education

THE FAMILY BACKGROUND

Charles Darwin was born on 12th February 1809 at The Mount in Shrewsbury. the home of his father Dr Robert Darwin. Dr Darwin was an eminent physician who had built up a successful medical practice. He struck an imposing figure, being six feet two inches tall and weighing over twenty-four stones. Such a man would obviously be impressive on his small son and in his early years Charles worshipped his father, 'the kindest man I ever knew'. Yet his wish to determine Charles's career led to an inner conflict of filial loyalty which may well have been a contributory factor to his later ill health.

Charles's grandfather, Erasmus Darwin, had been in his day a well-known figure — surgeon, naturalist and poet. His most famous book, *Zoonomia,* had contained evolutionary ideas. Charles in later life scorned his grandfather's work as being too vague and having little or no scientific facts to back up the arguments. In spite of this it would obviously have been an early influence in directing the young man's thoughts.

His mother was a daughter of Josiah Wedgwood, founder of the famous pottery firm. She died in 1817 when Charles was eight. Her death affected him deeply though he admitted later that he could remember little of her. He had one younger and three older sisters and his only brother, Erasmus, was five years his senior.

SCHOOL AND UNIVERSITY LIFE

At the age of eight he was sent to school in Shrewsbury, first as a day-boy to the school of the Rev. G. Case, a Unitarian minister, then, after a year as a boarder, to Shrewsbury School. Though a boarder, he was so near he found the slightest excuse to come home. The education at Shrewsbury was strictly classical, with a smattering of geography and history, and he derived little if anything from it. He was marked down as an ordinary boy who showed little promise of success. Charles, at this time, was a severe disappointment to his father. As a young boy he earned the rebuke: 'At your age it is high time you took yourself seriously. You care for nothing but shooting dogs and rat catching and you will be a disgrace to yourself and your family.'

Paternal conflict was not unknown in the Darwin family. Dr Robert Darwin's career had been decided upon by his father even though he had little enthusiasm for medicine. As a young man he had swooned at the sight of blood and surgery was always distasteful to him. Yet in spite of his own experience Dr Darwin determined that his son should become a doctor.

With this end in view he was taken away from Shrewsbury in 1825 at the age of sixteen and sent to Edinburgh University to begin his medical studies. Here he turned out to be as mediocre as at Shrewsbury. He was not helped by some extremely dull teachers but he could not raise any enthusiasm. Like his father he had little stomach for blood; he was forced to leave the operation he witnessed at Edinburgh and the memory haunted him for years.

He still indulged, however, in his boyhood hobby of collecting insects and shells. He spent more hours in the museum at Edinburgh studying marine life than attending lectures for his medical course.

It was obvious that Charles would never make a doctor. However, Dr Darwin remained determined that his younger son should become something in the world. It seemed as if his elder son, Erasmus, was going to become a member of the idle leisured class. Therefore, Charles would be sent to Cambridge to read for a degree to enable him to enter the Church. Charles did not really wish to become a country parson — he did not really know what he wanted — but a country vicarage would be pleasant enough, shooting and collecting beetles after performing the necessary duties of a clergyman.

For this purpose he entered Christ's College in December 1827. He did not attempt honours and just did enough work to ensure a creditable pass degree, finishing tenth in the list of candidates when he sat his final examination in January 1831.

The three years spent at Cambridge were in Charles's opinion wasted as 'completely as at Edinburgh as at School'. As soon as classes were over he went out to sing, drink and play cards with a group more intent on having a good time than determined to pursue their academic

John Stevens Henslow (1796-1861) was Professor of Botany at Cambridge while Darwin was studying to enter the Church, and Darwin was an enthusiastic companion of the professor on fieldwork.

studies. However, he did develop two interests that were to stand him in good stead later in his career, shooting and beetle collecting. He even went so far as to practise firing blanks in his room.

As for beetle collecting, Darwin whipped up sufficient enthusiasm amongst his friends to form a beetle brigade. One day he happened to pick up a catalogue of British insects and under the illustration of a rare beetle he had discovered was the caption, 'Captured by C. Darwin Esq.'. 'No poet ever felt more delighted at seeing his first poem in print than I', he later wrote.

This interest, though, was a mere hobby; he had no intention of classifying or dissecting the insects he had discovered. However, it did lead him to take natural history and geology a little more seriously and above all it led to the friendship of J. S. Henslow, Professor of Botany at Cambridge. Henslow liked taking students on fieldwork and inviting them home afterwards to discuss their work. Henslow was delighted with Darwin's enthusiasm and often asked him to accompany him on walks — so much so that he became known as 'the man who walks with Henslow'.

OPPORTUNITY TO EXPLORE

On 29th August 1831, on his return from a tour of North Wales, Darwin found two letters awaiting him. Both were from Cambridge professors, Peacock and Henslow, and both invited him to join HMS *Beagle* as the official naturalist on an expedition to survey the coasts of South America under the command of Captain Fitzroy. Darwin was speechless with joy, but his father was not happy about the venture. His father did suggest that if a man of common sense could be found who advised Charles to go he would not stand in his way. Such was his devotion to his father that he promptly wrote a letter to Henslow declining the invitation. In despondency he drove over to Maer, the home of his uncle Josiah Wedgwood, for the beginning of the shooting season. Here Darwin told his uncle of the offer and the latter was so enthusiastic that Darwin should go that they drove back to Shrewsbury at once. At Shrewsbury Uncle Josiah demolished Dr Darwin's arguments one by one and as he had always claimed that his brother-in-law was the most sensible man he had ever known there was nothing he could do but give his consent.

Thus by a single stroke of fortune — one man had already turned down the offer and Henslow himself had only been deterred by the strong opposition of his wife — he had been invited, though virtually unknown and ill qualified, to join an important voyage of scientific discovery where his hobby would be transformed into a life-long interest and devotion which would bring about as great a revolution in human thought as had Newton and Aristotle before him.

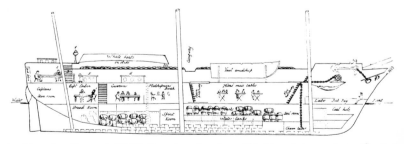

A side elevation of HMS Beagle, showing: (1) Darwin's seat in Captain Fitzroy's cabin; (2) his seat in the poop cabin; (3) his drawers in the poop cabin; (4) the azimuth compass; (5) the captain's skylight; (6) the gunroom skylight.

The voyage of HMS Beagle

THE MEETING WITH CAPTAIN FITZROY

On 5th September 1831 Darwin met Fitzroy for the first time. He at once took to this forthright and aristocratic figure. This is strange because by nature and training they were opposed. The Darwins were upper-class Whigs, the Fitzroys aristocrats and Tories. Darwin admired the manner and bearing of the man. It was obvious that everyone respected him and it would be obvious that on board ship his would be the authoritative voice. Yet already there was a sign of the fits of depression that were to end in his suicide some thirty-four years later.

It is often supposed that Darwin's beliefs in the literal interpretation of the Bible played a significant part in his selection by Fitzroy, who wished the voyage of the *Beagle*, amongst other things, to prove the Bible right. It now seems clear that the reason for Darwin's choice was a scientific one. Fitzroy at this time had no religious beliefs (his religious conversion was to come on his return to England) and he wished Darwin on board as a geologist and for no other purpose.

Darwin at this time was twenty-two years of age, some four years younger than Fitzroy. He presents a picture of a happy, perfectly assured young man. This figure, athletic and vigorous, would finally win Fitzroy over to accepting him as the naturalist on the *Beagle*, despite at first being somewhat alarmed at the shape of Darwin's nose.

DARWIN'S FIRST EXPERIENCE OF THE TROPICS

After the initial excitement it was to prove a long wait until the *Beagle* finally sailed on 27th December 1831. These three months of waiting were to prove 'the most miserable that I ever spent'. At this time he experienced the first signs of the illness that was to plague him for most of his life. A rash broke out on his hands and he experienced painful palpitation about the heart. He feared to go to a doctor lest he had to withdraw from the voyage. These pains were in all probability of neurotic origin brought on by stress at the thought of the voyage ahead.

At sea the pains were forgotten. He was treated by the hands of the ship as a land lubber and often had his leg pulled, but for all that he got on very well with them.

After a brief stay at the Cape Verde Islands they reached Bahia on 28th February 1832. Darwin was immediately excited by the tropics. On 18th March they sailed down the coast to Rio de Janeiro where they arrived on 3rd April. Now he could work. Within three days he had arranged a trip to a coffee plantation a hundred miles to the north. A party of seven was formed. They followed the coast for a few days and then turned into the tropical forest. Darwin was enthralled by it all — plants, birds, insects, the very colour and smell of the jungle.

The whole scene was beautiful, yet somehow terrifying. One day he witnessed a fight to the death between a Pepsis wasp and a large spider. He also saw a march of army ants, a black mass some hundred yards long devouring everything in its path. Everywhere he looked he was reminded of the law of the jungle — to prey and be preyed upon.

What he witnessed on this journey of the condition of the native Indian made his abhorrence of slavery greater than when he left England. This nearly brought to an abrupt end his relationship with Fitzroy. Back on board Darwin broached the subject of slavery. To Fitzroy slavery was part of the natural order. An argument ensued resulting in Darwin's being asked to leave the ship. Fortunately, after the fit of temper was over, Fitzroy immediately relented and invited Darwin back.

In any case they were to be parted for the next few months. Fitzroy was to sail northwards while Darwin stayed at Rio with Augustus Earle,· the official artist of the voyage, and Midshipman King. These were to be happy days spent in collecting specimens with, no doubt, Earle painting them before dispatching them to Henslow in Cambridge.

When the *Beagle* returned it brought the sad news that three of the crew had died from fever. So it was a low-spirited company that set sail for the virtually unknown lands of Patagonia and Tierra del Fuego. To add to this Darwin was seasick. He never became a sailor and was often incapacitated through severe bouts of seasickness. Generally, however, he stayed in good healthy condition.

(Facing page) A case of beetles collected by Darwin at various times.

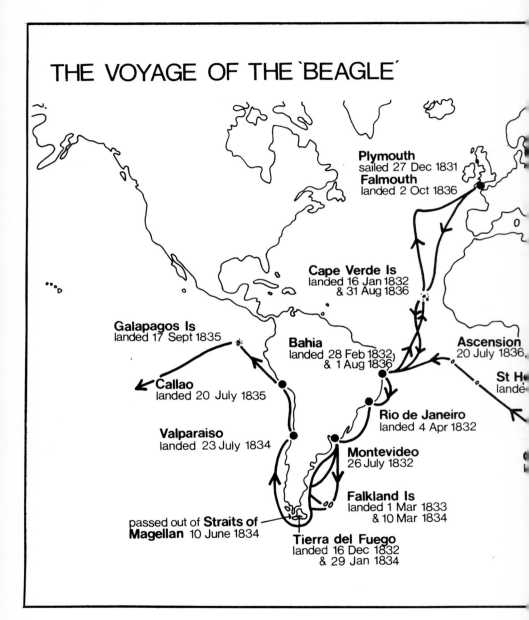

THE VOYAGE OF THE `BEAGLE´

Plymouth
sailed 27 Dec 1831
Falmouth
landed 2 Oct 1836

Cape Verde Is
landed 16 Jan 1832
& 31 Aug 1836

Galapagos Is
landed 17 Sept 1835

Bahia
landed 28 Feb 1832
& 1 Aug 1836

Ascension
20 July 1836

St H
landé

Callao
landed 20 July 1835

Valparaiso
landed 23 July 1834

Rio de Janeiro
landed 4 Apr 1832

Montevideo
26 July 1832

Falkland Is
landed 1 Mar 1833
& 10 Mar 1834

passed out of **Straits of Magellan** 10 June 1834

Tierra del Fuego
landed 16 Dec 1832
& 29 Jan 1834

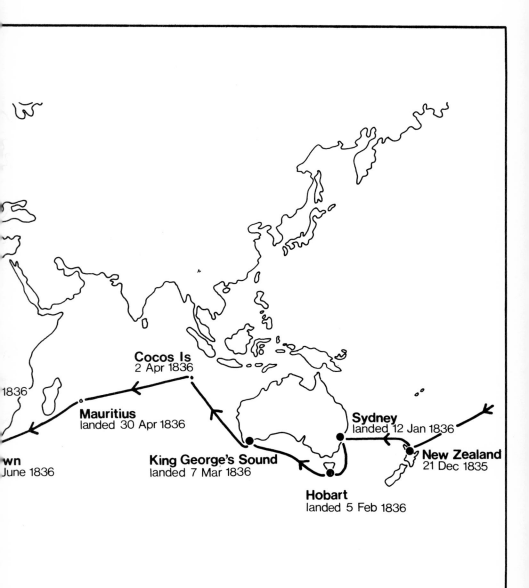

Cocos Is
2 Apr 1836

1836

Mauritius
landed 30 Apr 1836

wn
June 1836

King George's Sound
landed 7 Mar 1836

Sydney
landed 12 Jan 1836

New Zealand
21 Dec 1835

Hobart
landed 5 Feb 1836

EXTINCT ANIMALS

On 7th September 1832 they arrived at Bahia Blanca, four hundred miles south of Buenos Aires. It was a bleak and desolate land. Nearby, at Punta Alta, was to be the scene of some of Darwin's greatest discoveries. On the coastline, in a low bank some twenty feet in height, he found fossilised bones scattered over an area of some two hundred square yards. He was not quite sure what he was unearthing. The remains — tusks, teeth, claws — all came from bigger animals than any that Darwin knew.

What Darwin unearthed would obviously make him ponder over the creation of species. Was this proof that species were constantly changing and developing? It began to seem that creation was a continuous process and the earth had not been formed by some cataclysmic event in the year 4004 B.C. as most people believed in the mid nineteenth century.

TIERRA DEL FUEGO

At the end of November 1832, with everything now going well on the voyage, they set sail for Tierra del Fuego. Here the climate was appalling. The *Beagle* arrived in midsummer, yet for one month she was battered by raging seas. The land itself was cold, bleak and inhospitable. Yet to Fitzroy this was an essential visit.

Fitzroy had been in these waters before, in 1826. On that occasion one of his whale boats had been stolen. In reprisal he seized a native family as hostages. The adults soon escaped overboard leaving Fitzroy with several children. He kept a boy and a girl but managed to persuade an Indian family to take back the others. Later two men, one of whom died of smallpox in England, came on board and insisted on staying as substitute captives.

It was these three natives, Fuegia Basket, Jemmy Button, and York Minster, whom Fitzroy was determined to take back to their native land. In their years in England they had been 'civilised'. They had learnt the English language, had mixed in society, even being presented to King William IV, and had been taught the rudiments of the Christian religion. Now armed with supplies from the London Missionary Society and helped by a missionary, Richard Matthews, they were to bring the light to the dark ignorant peoples of Tierra del Fuego.

FUEGIA BASKET. 1833.

JEMMY'S WIFE 1834.

JEMMY IN 1834.

JEMMY BUTTON IN 1833.

YORK MINSTER IN 1833.

YORK IN 1833.

Fuegia Basket, Jemmy Button and York Minster were three natives of Tierra del Fuego who had been brought to England by Fitzroy in 1826. They were taken home aboard HMS Beagle in the hope that they might civilise their countrymen.

15

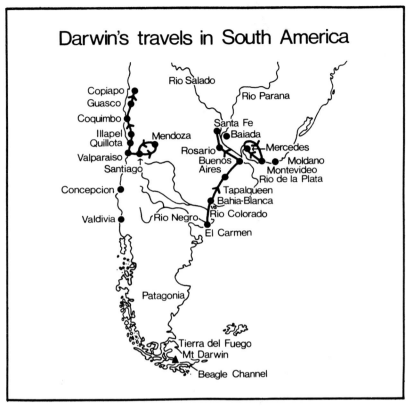

Darwin's travels in South America

Darwin at once was sceptical of the success of this venture. The people looked sullen, more like animals in appearance than men. They painted their faces and shaved their eyebrows and beards with sharp shells. Apart from a short mantle over the shoulders they went naked. They slept on the floor and they cultivated nothing, living mainly off fish. Somehow they survived and had grown accustomed to the conditions. Darwin noted in particular one incident soon after their arrival when a native woman came through curiosity to observe the *Beagle* and sat in a canoe suckling a child quite untroubled by the sleet falling on her naked breast.

So it was with some gloom and foreboding that Darwin and Fitzroy left the party under Matthews's charge to settle a colony in order to explore the surrounding terrain. They were away ten days. During this time the party had a narrow escape when a chunk of a glacier broke off and fell into the sea. The waves caused by the crash threatened to swamp and wash away their boat, but thanks to the prompt action of Darwin and two sailors the boat was secured. They were over a hundred miles from the *Beagle* and Fitzroy in gratitude named the peak under which they had camped 'Mount Darwin'.

On their return to the encampment they found Matthews in great distress. All his goods had been pillaged and it seemed they had arrived just in time to save his life. He was taken on board and later settled in New Zealand as a missionary.

Fitzroy was obviously upset, but he still thought that York Minster and Jemmy Button might accomplish the impossible and bring about the conversion of these people. However, when they returned some twelve months later they found the camp in ruins. York Minster and Fuegia had gone off and joined the wild Fuegians. Jemmy had remained and came to see them on the *Beagle,* but he too had returned to his former primitive way of life.

THE PAMPAS AND BUENOS AIRES

Disappointed, Fitzroy sailed north via the Falkland Islands to the mouth of the Plate. Fitzroy from this time became more and more morose and difficult to deal with. Darwin, on the other hand, became more self-confident. Ideas of becoming a country clergyman receded into the back of his mind. He had now dedicated himself and his life's work to natural science. Life had become full of interest for him.

In July 1833 the *Beagle* sailed for El Carmen in Patagonia. This was a wild, unexplored region. The natives were a fierce, aggressive people who were engaged in a struggle with the Argentinians who wanted their grazing lands. They were now, for the most part, wandering homeless over the plains.

Darwin's plan was to ride over the pampas to the Colorado where at Bahia Blanca he would rejoin the *Beagle*. If all was well he would continue his proposed journey to Buenos Aires.

Darwin was provided with a guide and a small bodyguard and set off on 11th August 1833. On his travels to the Colorado he came across the camp of General Rosas, the Argentinian army leader. Here again he witnessed appalling cruelty to the Indian population. If an Indian village were found inhabited wholesale massacre was the usual practice. The prettier females were usually spared, only to become concubines for the officers.

On 24th August Darwin met the *Beagle* in Bahia Blanca. He wanted to continue to Buenos Aires and did so. Again we are aware of a young man very much alive. He lived for the freedom of the open countryside, of being able to camp where he liked. He had enormous energy. He attempted to climb every mountain in sight. When one of the gauchos' horses went lame he offered him his own horse. He seemed to thrive on a diet of raw meat with the occasional delicacy of an ostrich egg. On one occasion he went twenty hours without water and when he arrived in Buenos Aires after forty days in the wilderness he was as hard and leathery as the gauchos themselves.

INTO THE PACIFIC

On 7th December 1833 the *Beagle* set sail, bound via Tierra del Fuego for the Pacific. The journey around Cape Horn was rough. It was winter and bitterly cold. The rigging froze and the decks were covered in snow. Rowlett, the purser, died as a result of the difficult conditions. It was, therefore, a gloomy ship that entered Valparaiso on 22nd July 1834. At least, after several months of bad weather and monotonous food, they were back in civilisation.

Soon Darwin was off exploring in the Andes. He relished the sensation of being at a high altitude. The air was so rare that one could see for miles. They were so high that potatoes would boil but would not cook. At night they had to huddle together for warmth. The chief interest lay not so much in animals as in the geology of the area. At twelve thousand feet he discovered fossilised sea shells, and lower down a petrified forest of trees. At last the geological history of America was beginning to fit into place. Once these trees had been on the shores of the Atlantic. At one time they had been submerged only to be raised up again through volcanic action. Geological history was one of continual movement and change.

He got back to the *Beagle* elated by these discoveries only to find Fitzroy half out of his mind. Earlier, to facilitate the voyage, Fitzroy had purchased a second ship, the *Adventure,* at his own expense. Now the Admiralty had refused to reimburse him. He must dismiss the extra

(Above) The Beagle laid ashore for repairs at Santa Cruz.

(Below) The ruins of the cathedral at Concepcion, Chile, demolished in six seconds by an earthquake in 1835.

sailors and sell the ship. This was a blow to his pride. He had thoughts of suicide. He was positive that he would abandon command and return home. In this situation Darwin remained perfectly calm. With the other officers he persuaded Fitzroy to continue. There was no need to sail again via Tierra del Fuego, they could more easily return by the Cape of Good Hope. Gradually Fitzroy was won round. The *Adventure* was sold for a good price of £1,400 and the *Beagle* made ready to sail again.

It was about this time that Darwin became ill after being bitten by a Benchuca bug. It was over a month before he fully recovered. The bite often gives rise to an infection known as Chagas disease. This has often been cited as the cause of Darwin's later sickness, but it is now commonly agreed that the predominant cause of this was probably neurotic, as we shall see later.

For the next few months they sailed along the Chilean coast and on 20th February 1835 anchored off Valdivia. Darwin went with little delay on one of his usual forays inland. While he was sitting on the ground he felt the whole earth tremble. There had obviously been an earthquake, but it was not until they later entered the port of Tahahiano that they realised the full horror. Debris was strewn everywhere. Concepcion was demolished in six seconds. The earth had visibly moved and in consequence the waterline was now clearly several feet lower than before. Here then was the proof that land could rise above sea level and an explanation as to why fossils of sea creatures could be found several thousands of feet above sea level.

Despite the calamity of the earthquake it had the effect of cheering up the crew of the *Beagle*. No doubt they felt themselves lucky to be alive and in a cheerful and relaxed mood they set sail for Valparaiso on 7th March 1835. Here Darwin had his last major excursion into the interior of South America.

It was now nearly four years since they had left England. At last Darwin began to feel the pangs of homesickness. He had been working and travelling hard for the whole voyage. He was beginning to feel tired and in need of a rest. No doubt it was with relief to all the company that they set sail on the homeward journey on 7th September 1835.

THE GALAPAGOS ISLANDS

As they sailed into the Pacific no doubt Darwin reflected on the

Charles Island (above) and Chatham Island (below), two of the Galapagos Islands where the Beagle arrived in September 1835. It was this visit, when Darwin observed how in each island the fauna had adopted differently to make the most of the surroundings, that was perhaps the most vital in his formulation of the theory of evolution.

21

events of the voyage so far. In one sense his most absorbing work and discovery had been in relation to the earth and its movement. Even with animals his most interesting discovery to date had been with extinct species. Yet his vast collection of animals and insects was his absorbing passion and by now his mind was beginning to turn to nature and the origin of life. It was to be the Galapagos Islands, where they landed on 16th September 1835, which were to prove the most singular and worth-while experience of the whole voyage.

The islands were mainly deserted and quite barren. They were occasionally visited by American whalers for postal services. Here they cruised a month, Darwin and some sailors being dropped off to explore at each island in turn.

The most interesting week was spent on James Island. The first creatures to capture their attention were marine lizards on the shore. Everything about them seemed odd: they never ventured inland further than ten yards; they were excellent swimmers and fed mainly on seaweed, yet they hated the water and lived mainly on land.

Other creatures were just as strange. There were flightless cormorants, penguins, and seals, both these last cold-water creatures, yet here they were in tropical waters. Inland they came across giant tortoises that would easily bear the weight of a man. They were so big and heavy that it was impossible to lift them or even turn them on their sides.

The birds were very tame. Never having seen man before, they regarded Darwin as just another animal and thought nothing of his presence. No animal seemed to prey off another. Darwin noticed lizards and birds eating off the same tree.

After this visit and several like it to other islands Darwin began to be struck by the uniqueness of the species. The islands were only fifty to sixty miles apart yet each island had its own species. There were interesting varieties of finches. Successive generations had adjusted themselves accordingly to the local habitat of each island. The most noticeable feature was the difference of beaks. On one island they had evolved strong beaks for cracking nuts, whilst on another the beak was smaller to allow the bird to catch insects; another was adjusted to feeding on fruit and insects.

With this evidence his mind began to be disturbed with startling new theories. Here he had met the most serious challenge to the idea of

A giant land tortoise of the Galapagos Islands. These creatures were so large that they could easily bear the weight of a man.

unchangeable species. The Galapagos Islands had probably been raised out of the sea by volcanic action. The birds would probably arrive first from South America. Then the reptiles would arrive, probably emerging from sea creatures. Primitive beasts like those he had dug up in South America had died out because they could not adapt to the environment. The finches on Galapagos had survived because they had been able to adapt to the varying habitat, as well as having no competitors from native birds already established there. If there had been, then no doubt these finches would have died out. It was these ideas of the mutability of species, of competition in the struggle for survival and the inescapable fact that somehow man was linked to this chain of development that began to shake the confidence and serenity that Darwin had gained during the voyage.

Obviously the ideas outlined above did not present themselves to

Darwin immediately in that form but as the *Beagle* made for home he would naturally ponder on what he had witnessed.

COCOS ISLAND

There was to be one more important stop on the way home to furnish Darwin with yet more evidence for the theories he was already formulating. This was at Cocos Island in the Indian Ocean. Here again he witnessed animals adapting to the environment. Darwin saw crabs that could crack and eat coconuts, dogs that could catch fish, and fish that lived off coral.

It was here, too, that he formulated his theory of the formation of coral islands. If land could rise out of the sea, so Darwin thought, it could also sink. Coral could not live below 120 feet. If dead coral existed below this level, then it would suggest that the land was sinking and taking the coral formation with it.

Darwin went out with Fitzroy and took soundings which proved that coral did exist below 120 feet. Here then probably lay the proof that coral formation was an end product of centuries of a slow reciprocal process. On one hand the land was raised out of the sea by violent activity. The land thus raised up would be colonised by coral formations around the coastline, and when the land again sank into the sea the coral would sink with it, leaving a massive coral reef around where the island once was.

After this last major scientific discovery they paid one last brief visit to South America. They left here on 19th August 1836 and on 2nd October they arrived, after nearly five years, back home in Falmouth.

The development of a theory

HOME AND FAME

He wasted little time in getting back to Shrewsbury. He arrived there on 4th October, late at night. Although he had been away for five years he was too considerate to knock his family up, so he decided to stay the night at a hotel. The next day he walked to The Mount and amongst the general cries of welcome from the family his father was heard to exclaim: 'Why, the shape of his head is quite altered.' In one sense this physical change epitomised the difference of five years. He had left a likeable, robust young man, but with little idea of vocation. He returned a determined natural scientist.

The next two years were to prove to be amongst the busiest of Darwin's career. He soon began classifying his vast collection of specimens at Cambridge. As well, the voyage had brought him considerable fame. He was elected a Fellow of the Royal Geological Society of which he became secretary. In these years he was working hard writing up the voyage of the *Beagle* in five volumes. In 1839 he published his own journal of the voyage. Much to his surprise it became a best-seller.

MARRIAGE

At the end of January 1839 he married his cousin Emma Wedgwood, the youngest daughter of his favourite uncle Jos. As was his customary procedure he went into the question of marriage with deliberate calculation. He drew up a balance sheet of the advantages and disadvantages of the affair. There would, he argued, be interruptions to work; there would be children to provide for and necessary family visiting. Against these, and no doubt looking around his cheerless bachelor apartments, he thought of 'a nice soft wife on a sofa with a good fire and books and music perhaps'. Therefore the solution clearly presented itself: 'Marry, marry, marry Q.E.D.'

Emma was one year older than Charles. She was an attractive, gay-hearted and intelligent young woman who took a keen interest in music and was devoutly religious. It seems to have been a perfect match. Science did not interest her a great deal although Darwin for most of their married life was immersed in his work. Such was his deep devotion to her that Darwin never felt secure away from her. His trust was completely in her and in his long years of illness she was his greatest comfort. As has been noted, 'the perfect nurse had married the perfect patient'.

Shortly after their marriage they moved into rooms in Gower Street in London. Here, for a time, they entered London society. However, Darwin was already feeling that London with its busy streets and social duties was too much for him. He needed the quiet and solitude of the country. In 1842 they moved to Down House at Downe in Kent where they lived the remainder of their lives. In the same year as they moved to Downe he made an excursion into Wales. Only a few years previously he had been climbing every mountain in sight in South America. This was to be the last time he was to feel strong enough to climb a mountain. From 1838 the life of this vigorous and seemingly athletic man was to be dominated by ill health.

THE CAUSE OF DARWIN'S ILL HEALTH

The nature of Darwin's ill health has been the cause of much controversy. There have been many explanations offered. The effects of the voyage, with the regular bouts of seasickness and an irregular diet with much hard work, have been noted. As well he suffered a bite of the Benchuca bug on the voyage. In spite of the severity of these physical privations it seems more probable that the illness had its cause in a neurotic condition. Possibly it may have been psychosomatic in that he was punishing himself for going against his father's wishes, for in the years immediately following his return from the voyage of the *Beagle* he would be compelled to tell his father of his determination to become a scientist and not a clergyman. Perhaps the most acceptable theory is that the illness was caused by a deep neurotic disturbance awakened by the revolutionary ideas that were beginning to dominate his thinking. Darwin hated controversy yet he knew and feared that his ideas would not only be destructive of old scientific belief but would also challenge contemporary religious belief and in consequence

Emma Wedgwood married her cousin Charles Darwin in January 1839. The couple were devoted to each other, and Emma was the perfect nurse to her husband during his long illness.

threaten the stability of Victorian society.

In one sense his illness furthered his work; his life became centred on Downe. A visit to London would mean several days of recuperation. Even a chance meeting with a neighbour might mean a sleepless night. Therefore to avoid undue interruption as much as possible Darwin avoided meeting people and kept firmly to an accepted routine.

DARWIN'S ROUTINE

The routine which he kept for most of his life began before breakfast with a walk, usually in the Sand-walk. After breakfast he began work at 8 a.m. and considered the one and a half hours until 9.30 a.m. the best period for working. At 9.30 he would break off from work and come into the drawing-room to read the morning's correspondence, as well as having the family letters read to him. At 10.30 he would return to the study and work until 12 noon.

Work was now over and the rest of the day was given over to exercise, reading and resting. The evening consisted of a session of having a novel read to him or of heavier scientific matter which he would read to himself. Perhaps after listening to his wife playing the piano he would go to bed about 10 o'clock.

EARLY WORKS AND THE BEGINNING OF A THEORY

The years immediately after his marriage were occupied in completing his work on the *Beagle*, publishing his findings on the formation of coral reefs in 1842, and in 1844 his *Geological Observations on the Volcanic Islands*. In 1846 Darwin began his work on barnacles, which was to occupy him fully for eight years.

As early as 1837 he had opened his notebooks on the mutability of species. At first this was kept a secret to himself. No doubt he confided first to his wife and then to his closest friends, Charles Lyell and Joseph Hooker, the famous botanist.

It was obvious that man had selected and improved the stock of his domestic animals. To understand the working of breeding he joined local pigeon fanciers' clubs and studied the form and pedigree of race

---

(Facing page) Charles Darwin at the time of his marriage.

horses. If man can improve stock, then how can nature of its own accord improve, was the question that remained to be answered.

In 1838 Darwin read for amusement Malthus's *Essay on Population*. Malthus's main point was that man is abundantly fertile, much more so than the world is equipped to satisfy his needs. To avert the threat of overpopulation man's numerical growth is controlled by disease, famine and war.

At once Darwin connected the grim message of Malthus into a theory of how nature herself selects. It was obvious that nature bred a vast over-supply of experiments. The failures were murdered, the successes survived, being the best adapted to the environment.

Not until 1842 did he dare commit these ideas to paper and then it was only a very brief account contained in a 35-page notebook. Two years later he wrote a fuller draft of 230 pages which contained a discussion of natural and unconscious sexual selection which is closely parallel to the eventual first part of the *Origin*.

What is missing from this is the reason why organisms of the same stock diverged. This still puzzled him. In a moment of inspiration in a coach near Downe the solution presented itself. It seemed 'that all dominant and increasing forms tend to become adapted to many and highly diversified places in the economy of nature'. The finches on the Galapagos Islands are an obvious example of this adaptation to the environment.

The theory was now taking shape, yet he was still reluctant to publish. As the years slipped by and his health did not improve he began to fear that death would cut short his work. Therefore he wrote a letter to his wife, to be opened only in the event of his death, instructing her to have the work edited and published.

His friends, Lyell and Hooker, continued to press Darwin to publish. Lyell urged Darwin to publish a brief sketch but Darwin was against this and proposed a book three to four times as big as *The Origin of Species* was eventually to be.

Also there was the thought of blasphemy delaying publication. He had been brought up to believe in the literal interpretation of the Bible. On board the *Beagle* he had been laughed at by his comrades for using the Bible as a touchstone in any moral dispute. Yet the further he researched the more obviously did the Genesis story appear little more than a myth.

Sir Joseph Hooker (1817-1911) was director of the Royal Botanic Gardens at Kew. A friend of Darwin, he urged him to publish his theory of evolution and defended him against criticism afterwards.

31

Professor T. H. Huxley (1825-95) had discounted the possibility of evolution before publication of 'The Origin of Species', but he then accepted the theory and became one of its most effective champions, earning himself the nickname 'Darwin's bulldog'.

He faced the horror of affronting his own family and the nation in their religious beliefs. The more effective the book became the more effective was the pain and horror. No wonder he felt 'haunted' by the idea of evolution and wrote to Hooker that he felt like someone 'confessing a murder'. Subconsciously at least he no doubt wished to postpone the dilemma, maybe to escape the consequence completely. However, events were to determine differently.

THE BOMBSHELL FROM WALLACE

As early as 1855 Darwin had noted in *Annals of Natural History* a paper on species by Alfred Russell Wallace bearing an alarming resemblance to his own ideas. Some two years later he received a letter from Wallace, who was in the Celebes Islands, on the question of the variety and breeding of domestic animals. Again these suggestions were similar to Darwin's own problems experienced earlier. He replied in somewhat cautious tones mentioning that he had been working on these ideas for the previous twenty years. There was to be another letter on animal distribution and then came the bombshell. While lying ill in bed from malaria, Wallace had arrived at much the same conclusion with regard to natural selection as Darwin. What Darwin had taken twenty years to work out Wallace had apparently formed in three.

At about this time his youngest son had died of scarlet fever. Darwin was prostrate with grief and he passed the matter into the hands of Lyell and Hooker. They proposed a compromise by the reading of a joint paper consisting of Wallace's letter and an extract of Darwin's ideas before the Linnaean Society. This was read on 1st July 1858 where it seems to have caused little excitement, possibly because of the difficult and novel material.

The danger of being forestalled was imminent. Darwin now agreed to go ahead and publish. He abandoned for the time being his big work and he agreed to publish a mere summary — *The Origin of Species.* This he accomplished in the space of thirteen months in spite of the usual symptoms of pain and nausea.

'THE ORIGIN OF SPECIES'

The first edition of *The Origin of Species* of 1, 250 copies was sold out on the day of publication. It immediately became the central document of all evolutionary theory. It may be asked why this was so and how Darwin himself, rather than Wallace for instance, became the pivot around which other evolutionists were content to gather. The answer lies in the main in the character of the man himself. He was a determined man and was insistent that all speculation must first of all be verified by a large and incontestable volume of facts. He was always unwilling to jump to conclusions. Again and again he would return to his store of facts to corroborate a conclusion already reached. Before evolution could be understood or accepted by the public at large it had to be prepared with a multitude of hard facts and the principle of natural selection had to be thoroughly analysed and its implication worked out. This is what Darwin performed and Wallace did not.

The essential doctrine of the book was that species change. This is achieved through natural selection of those species best suited to survive. Because the resources of nature are limited all life must engage in a struggle for existence in which only the most favoured will survive. Darwin argued that no two individuals are alike, all showing variation in some degree or other. Some species possess variations that prove helpful in this competition for survival. As a consequence these will produce the most offspring. Each subsequent generation will improve and maintain the characteristics of their parents and so gradually diverge further and further from the original stock. Eventually the new forms are so different from the original that they may be considered a new species.

When the storm broke over the *Origin* Darwin was away at Ilkley on a water cure. He maintained absolute silence and for the rest of his life stayed clear of open controversy. Darwin was always sensitive to criticism. Like most men he liked praise and was elated by it. Criticism brought on depression and a feeling of uncertainty. He had been pondering over the likely reception of the book for months, fearing a determined opposition. Yet he had powerful support from his friends Lyell and Hooker and a recent convert, T. H. Huxley.

At the famous debate of the British Association at Oxford in 1860 Huxley clearly had the better of the argument against the anti-Darwinians. From this meeting one can begin to date the beginning of the change in public opinion which would eventually accept evolution as fact. This acceptance was in many respects due to the championship of the cause by Huxley who quickly earned himself the nickname of

Down House at Downe in Kent where Darwin and his wife moved in 1842. He spent the rest of his life there and the peaceful surroundings greatly helped him in his work.

'Darwin's bulldog'.

The strongest criticism to the book came from scientists, zoologists and botanists who though they read the book were determined not to believe it. Even Lyell, although gloating over the general outline of the book, wanted Darwin to put more of divine direction in. This was, in the main, the sore point both with scientists and theologians. *The Origin of Species* seemed directly to challenge the Bible.

To most believers Darwin's conclusions meant not only the banishment of God as the creator and designer of the world but also that man, created in God's own image, was descended from a few primordial forms and incontrovertibly linked to the world of the beasts. Darwin had deliberately refrained from working out this conclusion in the *Origin* as he felt he was treading on too dangerous ground in attempting to analyse the 'sacred' animal. Obviously this study would have to be worked out, but always willing to stay clear of controversy he turned in the next few years to a study of 'safe' books.

considerations, which have thoroughly convinced me
that species have been modified, during a
long course of descent, by the preservation
or the natural selection of many successive
slight favourable variations. I cannot believe
that a false theory would explain, as it
seems to me that the the theory of natural
selection does explain, the several large
classes of facts above specified. It is a
valid objection that science as yet throws
no light on the far higher problem of the
essence or origin of life. Who can explain
what is the essence of the attraction of gravity? No
one now objects to following out the results
consequent on this unknown element of attrac-
-tion; notwithstanding that Leibnitz formerly
accused Newton of introducing "occult quali-
-ties & miracles into philosophy." —

Charles Darwin

p 514 3ᵈ Edit.
of "Origin"

Lines from Darwin's manuscript of 'The Origin of Species'.

The last years

A SERIES OF 'SAFE' BOOKS

It was no doubt with considerable relief that Darwin took up an earlier study of orchids. Orchids for a time became a part of his life as had barnacles been earlier. The eventual book, *The Various Contrivances by which Orchids are fertilised by Insects*, was published in 1862.

By this time his fame was spreading. On 30th November 1864 the Royal Society awarded Darwin the Copley Medal. Within a year there was a stampede of societies to press decorations upon him. He was elected an honorary member of the Berlin Academy as well as the Royal Medical Society and the Royal Society in Edinburgh. What gave him most pleasure was the confirming of an honorary LL.D by his old university of Cambridge in 1877. Despite his obvious love of being thus honoured he sometimes mislaid his diplomas and forgot to which societies he belonged.

FAMILY LIFE

In spite of this increasing fame his family life went on with little disturbance. As a father Darwin was always kind, rarely scolding and liking his children near him. Often when they were sick he would have them tucked up on a sofa in the study. On one occasion his son Leonard was found jumping off the furniture. He was rebuked by his father but Leonard simply told him to go out of the room. On another occasion his young daughter tried to bribe him with a sixpence to leave his work and go out and play. Obviously at the back of his mind was the memory of his own boyhood and he was determined not to be the cause of such pain and anguish as he had experienced.

The origin of man was still kept in the background and for his next study he turned his attention to climbing plants. *The Movements and Habits of Climbing Plants* was published in the journal of the Linnaean

Society in 1864 but not in book form until 1875. He could not resist stressing the evidence for natural selection. Plants have less mobility than animals, not because they are necessarily inferior, but because they are fixed to one spot they could derive no advantage from a greater mobility. After his next book, *The Variation of Animals and Plants under Domestication* (1868), which attempts an explanation of heredity, he turned at last to the subject of subjects.

'THE DESCENT OF MAN'

In 1871 Darwin worked on *The Descent of Man* without interruption and the following year it was published. It is usually considered his second most important book. It is divided into two halves, the first dealing with man while the second deals with natural and, in particular, sexual selection.

Darwin begins by drawing out the physical similarities between man and the apes. For example, the brain and sense organs were similar in composition, as were the hair and facial musculature. Both had no tail yet possessed a vestigial tail in embryo. There were also physiological similarities in reproduction, gestation, lactation and development. Also there were important resemblances in psychological characteristics, such as instinct and emotions, and as well he noted in apes and monkeys the germs of reason, imagination and morality.

Man's distinctive pre-eminence was due not to one characteristic but to many. First there was his upright position with the consequent freedom of movement. Then came the use of hands and above all his mental capacity which gave him control over tools and the use of language. Darwin thought of man's mind as a weapon evolved in the struggle for survival. Because of man's brain power there was a great difference between him and the apes, but this difference was of degree rather than of kind. However close man may be to the apes, it was not true to say that man had evolved from the monkey, but rather that they both had a common ancestor.

Having put man firmly in the company of the beasts he then turned to study sexual selection. He studied the use that animals made of ostentatious displays, colouring and size in order to win their respective mates. In a final chapter he dealt with sexual selection in man. Here he noted it was the female that attracted the male by facial beauty and attractive figure. Furthermore he noted that certain racial differences

A cartoon of Darwin from 'Hornet', 22nd March 1871. Darwin never implied that man is descended from apes, as has become the popular belief. What he suggested was that man and apes descended from a common ancestor.

The new study at Down House. If one of his children was ill, Darwin would have the child tucked up on the sofa while he worked.

in man were probably the outcome of sexual selection. For example, many negro tribes preferred the blackest-skinned women. Therefore, over a period of time would emerge a characteristic in accord with the sexual desires of the tribe.

Much to his relief the publication of *The Descent of Man* caused little storm. The battle over evolution had been largely won — Science, the Church and the public were in the main reconciled to it. After *The Descent* had been written Darwin said farewell to controversy. From now on he returned to the collection of facts and the observation of specimens. It is interesting to note that in these last years, with his two 'big' books behind him, his health improved considerably.

THE LAST BOOKS

In 1872 he published *Expressions of the Emotions in Man and Animals*. It was the first attempt to treat the subject from a purely naturalistic and evolutionary angle. One particular part of his work involved the testing of the emotions in man as to whether they were innate or had to be learned like a language. To this purpose he circulated a questionnaire to a number of people in different countries. From their answers he was able to draw the conclusion that the simpler emotions, for example rage, pleasure, sorrow and disgust, are innate, while the more sophisticated signs of emotion like kissing are largely determined by a person's social background and have to be learned or unconsciously acquired.

Having finished with man he went almost to the opposite end of the organic world and resumed his study of Drosera. To determine the advantage gained by the plant through the ability to eat flesh Darwin and his son Frank raised two sets of Drosera. One was fed on meat, the other was not. The meat-fed plants grew much stronger, thus suggesting that in its usual habitat of bog and marshy ground it had to have a meat diet in order to survive, through the lack of a normal diet. These findings were published as *Insectivorous Plants* in 1875. His next book *Power and Movement in Plants* (1880) was again written with the assistance of Frank.

In his last years he became absorbed in the life of the earthworm and in 1881 he published *The Formation of Vegetable Mould through the Action of Worms*. His son Horace constructed at Downe a 'wormstone' to calculate the rate at which objects sank into the ground. In due course he discovered that earthworms sank the stone at the rate of 2.22 millimetres a year. Such was his enthusiasm in this work that not only did he ask Frank to play the bassoon to earthworms to observe their reaction to sound but he even left the secure confines of his house and ventured as far as Stonehenge to observe how worms were the cause of the gradual sinking of the large stones. He was able to calculate that on every acre of the chalk hills near Downe worms brought up eighteen tons of earth annually. Thus every few years the soil of the English countryside was subject to a natural form of cultivation, being mixed and enriched in its passage through the bodies of earthworms.

HIS LAST ILLNESS AND DEATH

Darwin's final years were full of domestic happiness and financial prosperity. The sense of a need to work to prove a theory had now

41

departed. He became relaxed and with an improvement in health began to venture from the confines of Down House, visiting the Lake District on two occasions. Yet he began to find it difficult to work and concentrate over long periods. He gradually became aware of his own frailty. Close friends were beginning to die: Lyell died in 1875 and in August 1881 his elder brother Erasmus died. 'Life', he wrote to

(Above) This 'Wormstone' in the garden at Downe was constructed by Darwin's son Horace. It was discovered that the stone sank into the ground 2.22 millimetres annually because of the action of earthworms.
(Facing page) The Sand-walk at Downe where Darwin would stroll each morning before breakfast.

Wallace, 'has become very wearisome to me.'

Early in 1882 whilst visiting Romanes in London he suffered a heart attack. He recovered and in the spring he felt strong enough to go out alone and walk in the Sand-walk, but as a consequence he suffered another attack. He became very weak but he refused to be bed-ridden. On 15th April he was seized with giddiness at dinner and fainted before he could reach a chair. Three days later he woke Emma in the middle of the night with acute pain and fainted. In a calm period when the pain had eased and he had regained consciousness he turned to Emma and whispered: 'I am not in the least afraid of death.' These symptoms of fainting and sickness continued until on the morning of 19th April 1882 he died peacefully.

Emma and the children wanted him to be buried at Downe, but soon the Press, politicians and the Church decided that Westminster Abbey should be his final resting place. The controversial author of *The Origin of Species* had now become part of the establishment. In great pomp, so remote from his daily life, with Huxley, Hooker, and Wallace, as well as two dukes, an earl and the President of the Royal Society as his pall-bearers, he was laid to rest beside Sir Isaac Newton, the only other English scientist worthy of comparison.

To some people it is surprising that Darwin should hold so pre-eminent a place in the history of Science. Neither at school nor at university did he show sign of academic promise. Later in life he lived the life of a semi-recluse, hating to appear in public. His speech was slow and he disliked conversation, often coming out worse in an argument.

Yet he ranks with the great thinkers of the world, principally because of the unrelenting pursuit of the one idea which dominated his life — evolution by natural selection. To prove this one idea went literally hundreds of facts, observed, analysed and categorised. Through this selfless search over fifty years he brought about as great a change in human thought as had occurred since time began.

THE PRINCIPAL EVENTS OF DARWIN'S LIFE

1809   Darwin born at Shrewsbury
1817   Goes to the Rev. G. Case's school at Shrewsbury. Death of his mother
1818   Goes to Shrewsbury School
1825   Enters Edinburgh University
1827   Admitted to Christ's College, Cambridge
1830   Lyell's *Principles of Geology*
1831   Graduates from Cambridge and on 27th December sets sail on HMS *Beagle*
1832   Travels mainly in Brazil and the tropical forests. *The First Reform Bill*
1833   Explores region of Tierra del Fuego and the Plate. *The abolition of slavery*
1834   The *Beagle* sails into the Pacific
1835   Travels in Chile and the Galapagos Islands
1836   Arrives home at Falmouth
1837   Settles in London. Starts work on *Origin*
1838   Read Malthus *On Population*
1839   Married. *Journal of Researches* published
1842   Moves to Down House. First draft of *Origin*
1844   Fuller version of *Origin*
1846   Began to work on barnacles
1848   His father dies
1856   Urged by Lyell and Hooker to publish his theory of evolution
1858   Received Wallace's letter
1859   *Origin of Species* published
1860   The meeting of the British Association at Oxford.
1862   Published book on orchids
1864   Awarded the Copley Medal of the Royal Society
1868   Published *The Variations of Animals and Plants under Domestication*
1871   *Descent of Man* published
1872   *The Expressions of the Emotions in Man and Animals* published
1873   Contributed five papers to *Nature*.

1880   *The Power of Movement in Plants* published
1881   His last book published: *The Formation of Vegetable Mould through the Action of Worms*
1882   Darwin dies at Down House. Buried in Westminster Abbey

BIBLIOGRAPHY

Two of Darwin's works are readily available in paperback, *The Origin of Species* (Mentor) and *Journal of a Voyage* (Everyman). *The Autobiography* has been revised and edited by his granddaughter, Lady Barlow (Collins, 1958). *The Illustrated Origin of Species* by Charles Darwin, edited and abridged by Richard E. Leakey, was published by Faber in 1979.

Of the books on Darwin the one by his son Francis Darwin, *Darwin's Life and Letters,* is still worth consulting. More recent studies include: *Charles Darwin* by Gavin de Beer (Nelson, 1961); *Charles Darwin and his World* by Sir Julian Huxley and Henry Bernard Davies Kettlewell (Thames and Hudson, 1965); *Darwin and the Beagle* by Alan Moorehead (Penguin, 1970); and *The Beagle Record* by Professor R. D. Keynes (Cambridge University Press, 1978).

INDEX